1913: "Tiny" Broadwick becomes the first woman to parachute out of a plane.

1937: Sabiha Gökçen becomes the world's first female fighter pilot.

1958: Maria Teresa de Filippis is the first woman to drive in an F1 race.

I0806725

1964: Patti McGee wins the first Women's National Skateboard Championship.

1979: Sylvia Earle walks 1,250 feet (381 meters) under the sea—the deepest anyone has ever walked.

1989: Cindy Lee Van Dover joins the team of the deep-diving submersible *Alvin* as its first female pilot.

Curious?

Turn the page!

active minds®

BOOK of FIRSTS

Fearless Firsts

WHO was the world's first female fighter pilot?

WHY did the first person go over Niagara Falls in a barrel?

WHEN was the first woman inducted into the Skateboarding Hall of Fame?

WOMEN WHO LEAPED, JUMPED, AND FLEW

Written by
Dale Jones

sequoia® kids media
An imprint of PHOENIX International Publications, Inc.

Visit us at
SequoiaKidsMedia.com
for bonus downloadable content

Art © Shutterstock 2024 ghenadie; Borisovna.art; Shmer; Adi Klau; Lana Way; GoodStudio; NotionPic; Robert Adrian Hillman; Hetman Bohdan; Miloje; shurkin_son; Click Bestsellers; Futurodox; Sergey Ginak; Stephen B. Goodwin; Jarous; Joanna Dineva; Vixit; LIAL; Morarus; Alvins Creative; Vector Tradition; photofriday; Featureflash Photo Agency; ChristinaAiko Photography
© Wikimedia Commons 2024 Jaan Künnap (cover, pg 18); Albert Witzel (cover); NASA/Bill Ingalls (cover, pg 11); Master Sgt. Brian Bahret/U.S. Air Force (pg 6); Kokomo Daily Tribune (pg 6); Turkish Air Force (pg 7); BevinKacon (pg 7); Office of Naval Research/U.S. Navy (pg 9); NASA (pg 10); NASA/James Blair (pg 11); Francis J. Petrie Collection/Niagara Falls Public Library (pg 12); Niagara Falls Heritage Foundation Collection/Niagara Falls Public Library (pg 13); Kalem Company (pg 14, 15); Kalem Company/General Film Company (pg 15); Ketil3 (pg 16); MrWalkr (pg 16); Oldsport (pg 17); Jaan Künnap (pg 18); Rodriguemeriaux (pg 22); Ralph Arvesen (pg 22); NOAA Photo Library (pg 25); © Flickr 2024 General Negative Collection/State Archives of North Carolina (pg 6); San Diego Air and Space Museum Archives (pg 7); KQED QUEST (pg 8); Nick Ares (pg 17); Gerald Geronimo (pg 23)

Published by Sequoia Kids Media,
an imprint of Sequoia Publishing & Media, LLC

Sequoia Publishing & Media, LLC,
a division of Phoenix International Publications, Inc.

8501 West Higgins Road, Chicago, Illinois 60631
34 Seymour Street, London W1H 7JE
Heimhuder Straße 81, 20148 Hamburg

CustomerService@PhoenixInternational.com

www.SequoiaKidsMedia.com

Library of Congress Control Number: 2024933048

ISBN: 979-8-7654-0716-5

Table of Contents

Introduction

People have chased the latest **adrenaline-filled thrills** since the beginning of time. Being the first to do something is a huge point of pride for any adventurer. People climb mountains or jump out of planes. Others walk underwater or get behind the wheel of a fast car.

Some people make adrenaline their lives. They do dangerous and exciting sports. They might dream of becoming the best in the world or setting new world records. Others do dangerous and exciting things for their jobs.

Thrill-seekers prove that there are no limits to bravery. But in the past, it was mostly men who were credited with firsts. Some men have even said that women do not have a place in certain sports or jobs. But **fearless women** don't listen!

Women have been performing **fearless feats** just as long as men. Sometimes, their stories go untold. But they existed, and their bravery inspires the next generations of daredevils of all genders.

Take a look at some of the people who have stopped at nothing to **chase their dreams** and set new records in their fields!

Georgia "Tiny" Broadwick

April 8, 1893–August 25, 1978

First female parachutist

When **Georgia Broadwick** was born, she weighed just 3 pounds (1.4 kilograms). So her family nicknamed her **"Tiny."** She never grew out of it. Even as an adult, Broadwick was barely 5 feet (1.5 meters) tall and weighed 80 pounds (36.3 kg).

In 1907, Broadwick saw an air performance at the North Carolina State Fair. Daredevils jumped out of balloons and parachuted to the ground. She asked the owner if she could join and he said yes. She took her **first jump** in 1908, at the age of 15. Fans knew her as the "Doll Girl."

In 1913, a famous pilot offered to let her jump out of one of his airplanes. On June 21, she became the first woman to **parachute out of a plane**, floating 2,000 feet (610 m) to the ground. Later that same year, she would be the first woman to parachute into water.

Broadwick would make more than 1,000 jumps. It wasn't safe, or easy. She often broke bones and dislocated her shoulders. Sometimes, she got tangled in wires. But she loved the thrill.

Sabiha Gökçen

March 22, 1913–March 22, 2001

First female fighter pilot

Sabiha Gökçen was born to a very poor family in Bursa, Turkey. When she was just 12, she met the Turkish president. She asked him for help attending a boarding school. He was impressed at her initiative and offered to adopt her. He gave her the name Gökçen, which means "belonging to the sky."

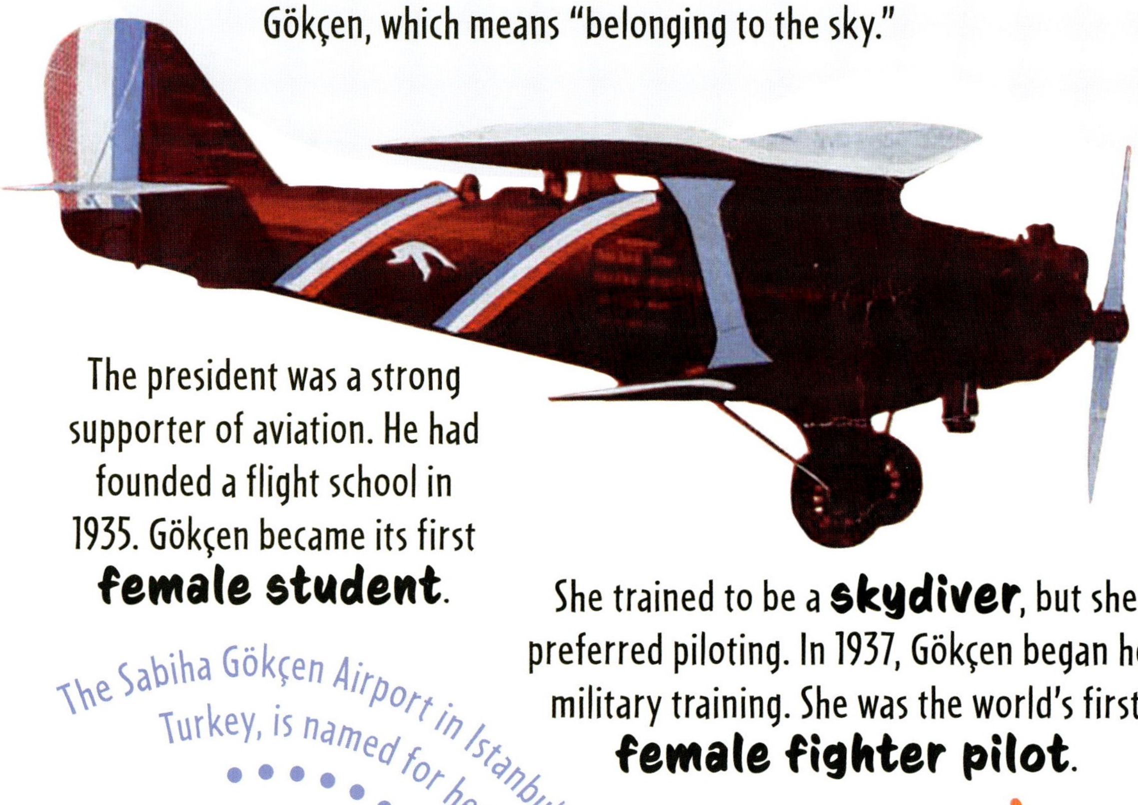

The president was a strong supporter of aviation. He had founded a flight school in 1935. Gökçen became its first **female student**.

She trained to be a **skydiver**, but she preferred piloting. In 1937, Gökçen began her military training. She was the world's first **female fighter pilot**.

The Sabiha Gökçen Airport in Istanbul, Turkey, is named for her.

Gökçen flew for over **8,000 hours** and took part in **32 combat missions**. In 1938, she started work as the chief trainer at the flight school. She trained men and women to fly planes.

Sylvia Earle

August 30, 1935–present

Led the first all-woman aquanaut team

When she was 13, **Sylvia Earle's** family moved to Florida. She loved exploring the plants and animals that lived in their waterfront backyard. In college, Earle studied botany. That's the study of plants. She learned how to **scuba dive** so she could see ocean plants up close.

In 1969, the US government built an underwater habitat off the coast of the Virgin Islands. It was about 50 feet (15.2 m) below the ocean's surface. They called it **Tektite**. The first mission sent four men underwater for 60 days. These men were called aquanauts.

Tektite didn't set out to hire women. But with **1,000 hours of dive experience**, it was hard to say no to Earle's application. She was hired as an aquanaut for *Tektite II*.

Earle led a team of five women to the habitat. They lived there for two weeks. It was their mission to see if people could safely live in dark, secluded spaces. They ate astronaut food for some meals. They spent 12 hours at a time diving in deep water. Their work paved the way for astronauts of all genders.

On September 19, 1979, Sylvia Earle set another record. She put on a special diving suit and walked on the seafloor. She was 1,250 feet (381 m) deep. This is the deepest underwater walk anyone has ever made.

Cindy Lee Van Dover

May 16, 1954–present

First and only female pilot of the deep-diving submersible *Alvin*

Cindy Lee Van Dover knew when she was a kid that she wanted to study the ocean. Her friends loved cats and dogs, but she loved horseshoe crabs. Her love led her to study hot springs deep under the ocean.

In 1985, she took her **first dive** on the submersible *Alvin*. Submersibles are underwater vehicles. They launch from ships and explore the ocean. *Alvin* took Van Dover 2 miles (3.2 kilometers) underwater off the coast of the Galapagos Islands, in the Pacific Ocean.

After she got her PhD in **deep sea biology** in 1989, she joined *Alvin*'s team. As a biologist, she might have had to wait years to have a project funded. But as the submersible's pilot, she could spend much more time at sea. She studied hard for nine months to earn her pilot's certification.

Van Dover was the leader of almost 50 dives in *Alvin*, and its **only female pilot**. In total, Van Dover traveled to the sea floor more than 100 times.

Alvin's deepest dive was 21,171.3 feet (6,453 m). That's nearly 4 miles (6.4 km)!

Susan Helms

February 26, 1958–present

First woman to live aboard the International Space Station

Susan Helms loved to fly. She was part of the first **Air Force Academy class** to train women, graduating in 1980. She tested and flew more than 30 different types of aircraft. Then, in 1990, she joined NASA.

Helms visited the **International Space Station (ISS)** in 2000. She helped prepare it for the first crewmembers. The next year, Helms went back as part of that second mission. She was the first woman to live inside. She spent 163 days aboard.

In 1993, Helms became the first woman from the US military to **go to space**. Over eight years, Helms went to space five times, spending a total of 211 days among the stars.

During that mission, Helms and fellow astronaut Jim Voss set a record for the **longest single space walk**. They spent 8 hours and 56 minutes outside the ISS.

Nicole Aunapu Mann

June 27, 1977–present

First Indigenous woman to go to space

Nicole Aunapu Mann is no stranger to danger. Mann is a colonel in the US Marine Corps. She served in combat missions to Iraq and Afghanistan. **She flew fighter jets**. And on October 5, 2022, she had the ultimate thrill—she went into space.

NASA chose Mann in June 2013. They sent her to the ISS in October 2022 as part of the SpaceX Crew-5 mission. Mann and her teammates lived and worked on the ISS for nearly six months. They performed tests and gave technology demonstrations.

In January 2023, Mann made her first **space walk**. She took her second in February, capturing a "space selfie" with her helmet camera. The second walk lasted 6 hours, 41 minutes. People watched her on YouTube.

Mann is a member of the Wailacki community. They are part of the Round Valley Indian Tribes in California.

Annie Edson Taylor

October 24, 1838–April 29, 1921

First person to go over Niagara Falls in a barrel

In 1901, 62-year-old **Annie Edson Taylor** was desperate. Her husband and son had died many years before. She didn't have a way of making money. Taylor needed a way to support herself. She wanted to do something that would make her famous.

Many people had gone through the Niagara rapids in a barrel. Taylor knew she'd have to outdo them. She decided to go **over the waterfalls** instead. It was risky. No one who had tried it before had survived.

She had a special barrel made to fit her body. There was a harness inside to hold her in place and prevent injuries. A heavy weight at the bottom of the barrel stopped it from rolling and kept it upright in the water.

On October 24, 1901, a crew took Taylor and her barrel out to the middle of the river. She climbed in. They put padding around her and sealed the top. They used a bicycle pump to put more air into the barrel so that Taylor had enough oxygen for her trip. Then, they set the barrel loose in the water.

It went over the falls and dropped into the churning water at the bottom. When it came up, it was intact. But it took another 20 minutes before Taylor was out of the barrel. She had bruises, a concussion, and a cut on her head. But she was alive!

Taylor is still remembered today as the **first person over the falls**. Circus performer Bobby Leach was the second. He tried it in 1911. He spent six months in the hospital afterward.

Today, there are heavy fines between $10,000 and $25,000 to discourage people from following in Taylor's footsteps.

Niagara Falls is between 167 and 188 feet (51 and 57.3 m) high.

Helen Gibson

August 27, 1892–October 10, 1977

First professional stuntwoman

In 1909, **Rose Wenger** saw a Wild West show go through her hometown. She decided that she wanted to work for one. In 1910, she joined another show. She learned how to do tricks with horses.

The season ended in California. Wenger started working as an extra and **stuntperson** for movie studios. Her first credited role was in the 1912 silent movie *Ranch Girls on a Rampage.* She became known for doing whatever it took to get the stunt done.

In 1914, she got a job as a stunt double in the show *The Hazards of Helen.* A couple of years later, the show's star, Helen Holmes, left. The producers asked Wenger to replace her. But they insisted she **change her name** to Helen. She did, and she took her husband's last name, Gibson.

For a time, Gibson was famous. But in the 1920s, Hollywood had fewer roles for women. Gibson went back to the Wild West show circuit, doing stunts on the side.

Gibson did her last stunt when she was almost **70 years old**. She drove a team of horses in the movie *The Man Who Shot Liberty Valence.*

Maria Teresa de Filippis

November 11, 1926–January 9, 2016

First female Formula 1 driver

Formula 1 (F1) is the top car racing series in the world. F1 began in 1950. The cars are small, with no roof and room for just one person. At first, **all the F1 drivers were men.**

In 1948, **Maria Teresa de Filippis** started racing cars. She moved up, driving in bigger races and faster cars. Ten years later, in 1958, she drove in an F1 race. She placed 10th in the Belgian Grand Prix. She also qualified for the French Formula 1 Grand Prix.

But de Filippis never got the chance to enter the race in France. The race director **didn't want a woman driver**. He banned her from the track. The next year, one of de Filippis's friends died racing. The loss led to her retirement.

Formula 1 wanted to make the sport more inclusive, so in 2023 it launched the F1 Academy. This is a junior-level series of races for young women.

De Filippis drove a Maserati 250F.

Women in the Driver's Seat

Today, there are no rules keeping women from F1. So far, though, there have only been **five** female drivers to attempt the Grand Prix level in all of F1 history. Only two have qualified for the races. The last one was in 1976. These five women were:

Maria Teresa de Filippis (1958)
Lella Lombardi (1974–1976)
Divina Galica (1976)
Desiré Wilson (1980)
Giovanna Amati (1992)

Jessi Combs

July 27, 1980–August 27, 2019

Set the women's land speed record

Jessi Combs was a professional car racer and thrill-seeker. In 2009, she was a host of the popular show ***MythBusters***.

In 2013, Combs got to drive the **North American Eagle Supersonic Speed Challenger**. She set a new record in women's four-wheel land speed racing. She drove at 398 miles (640.5 km) per hour. People called her "the fastest woman on four wheels."

The North American Eagle Supersonic Speed Challenger is 56 feet (17 m) long. It is powered by jets.

In 2019, Combs got the opportunity to get in the Challenger again. People wanted to see if she could beat the absolute women's **land speed record**. It was first set by Kitty O'Neil in 1976. O'Neal had driven a three-wheeled car at 512 miles (824 km) per hour.

But something went wrong. The car's front wheel failed, and the car crashed. Combs didn't make it out. Her team submitted her data for the world record. A year after her death, she was granted the Guinness World Record. She holds the women's land speed record at **522.783 miles (841 km) per hour**.

Junko Tabei

September 22, 1939–October 20, 2016

First woman to summit Mount Everest and complete the Seven Summits

Junko Tabei fell in love with mountains when she was growing up in Japan. In 1962, she graduated college and joined **mountaineering groups**. Most of these groups were made of men. They didn't think women should climb.

Tabei didn't let that stop her. She kept climbing. In 1969, she started a mountaineering club for women. She took her group to a mountain called Annapurna III in Nepal. It's one of the **most difficult mountains** in the world to climb. But they made it to the top. They were the first **all-woman group** to summit the mountain.

The motto of Tabei's ladies' climbing club was: "Let's go on an overseas expedition by ourselves."

In 1974, Tabei went back to Nepal. The next year, she was ready to tackle **Mount Everest**, the tallest mountain in the world. She succeeded! She was the first woman to do so. Through her lifetime, she participated in **44 all-female climbs**.

In 1992, Tabei was the first woman to complete the **Seven Summits**. That means she summited the highest mountain on all seven continents. She has also made it to the highest peaks of 76 different countries.

Tabei led her last climb in 2016. She had cancer, but she still managed to climb 10,170.6 feet (3,100 m) up **Mount Fuji**. Tabei passed away three months later, at the age of 77.

The Seven Summits

Mount Everest, Asia

Cerro Aconcagua, South America

Denali, North America

Mount Kilimanjaro, Africa

Mount Elbrus, Europe

Vinson Massif, Antarctica

Carstenz Pyramid, Oceania

Patti McGee

August 23, 1945–present

Won the first Women's National Skateboard Championship

Growing up in California, **Patti McGee** and her friends built their own skateboards. They steered them down hills and fell in love with "sidewalk surfing."

In 1964, McGee competed at the first Women's National Skateboard Championship. She won first place! She became the first **female professional skateboarder** and one of the first pros in the entire sport. She was the first skater to land a rolling handstand in competition.

The skateboard company Hobie paid her to travel and host demos and lessons. She showed off Hobie skateboards wherever she went. In 1965, she was on the cover of *LIFE* and *Skateboarder* magazines. She was the first woman to grace the skateboarding magazine's cover.

Commercial pre-made skateboards weren't sold until 1959.

In the late 1960s, McGee swapped sports. She took up downhill skiing. But she got back on a skateboard when she was 55!

In 2010, McGee was the first woman inducted into the **Skateboarding Hall of Fame**.

Khadijah Mellah

2000-present

First hijab-wearing jockey in a British horse race

When she was 12, **Khadijah Mellah** saw a flyer at her local mosque for the Ebony Horse Club in Brixton, England. She joined and fell in love with horses.

Mellah was chosen to ride in the Magnolia Cup in 2019. Her horse, **Haverland**, was not favored to win. But Mellah knew he could do it. The pair had a rocky start, but a burst of speed at the end of the race put Haverland in the lead. The victory meant Mellah was the **first hijab-wearing jockey** to ride in, and win, a British horse race.

After the race, Mellah was exhausted! On top of training, she had been studying for college exams and fasting for Ramadan.

Mellah's victory inspired the **Riding a Dream Academy**, which gives scholarships to young people from underrepresented backgrounds who want to ride horses. A film with the same name was made about Mellah in 2019.

Racehorses weigh around 1,200 pounds (544.3 kg). They can hit speeds of 44 miles (71 km) per hour. The average jockey weighs less than 120 pounds (54.4 kg). They must be fit to control the horse!

The Magnolia Cup is a **charity race** run every year. The jockeys are all women who work in fashion, business, or sports. Some of them don't have any riding experience at all! They're assigned a trainer and a horse. All the money made from the race is donated to charity.

Fun at the X Games

In 1995, the sports channel ESPN wanted to showcase extreme sports, like skateboarding, BMX biking, and street luge. They started the X Games. The games started with 27 events. Only six of them were for women. One other was for a paired man and woman. The first X Games was a hit!

The first Winter X Games was held in 1997. Extreme snowboarding, ice climbing, and snow mountain biking were a few of the events. In later years, they added events for skiing. At the 2023 **Aspen Winter X Games**, there were six events each for women and men.

Marie Martinod was part of the first freeskiing events at the 2014 Sochi Olympics.

The Olympics added its first **extreme sport**—snowboarding—to the 1998 Games.

Extreme Women

Over time, ESPN has changed which sports are featured at the Games. Women's competitions have often been the first to be cut. In 2023, only two events were for women, and they were both skateboarding. Women skateboarders are concerned about their future in the X Games. More and more have been working to support women in extreme sports.

Women on the Podium

In 2023, 13-year-old **Arisa Trew** competed in the Summer X Games. In the Pacifico Women's Skateboard Vert, she did a move called a **720**. For this trick, the boarder jumps and rotates the board twice while in the air before landing. It was the first time a woman had ever landed the move. She won the gold medal.

Reira Iwabuchi is a snowboarder. During the 2022 Olympics, she tried a move called the frontside triple cork 1260. The athlete both flips and rotates three times while in the air. She nearly got it. The next year, though, she was able to pull it off at the X Games! Iwabuchi was not the first person to land the move. But she was **the first person to do it in competition**. She won the gold medal that year.

Ashley Fiolek was born Deaf. She never let anything get in her way. Growing up, she did ballet, played basketball, and ran track. When she was just three years old, her parents gave her a kid's motorcycle. She went on to ride **motocross**. Riders take motorcycles through rough terrain and an obstacle course. In 2009, she won a medal in motocross at the X Games. She was the first **Deaf medalist** in X Games history.

Taylor Swift

December 13, 1989–present

The Eras Tour consisted of **151 shows over five continents**.

First person to earn more than $1 billion in tour sales

Some people get butterflies giving a report in front of the class or reading lines in front of friends and family. Imagine performing in front of a packed stadium of 72,000 screaming fans. **Taylor Swift** did that every night during her **Eras Tour**.

When Swift found out the original recordings of her songs were sold without her knowledge, she took control. She began re-recording her albums and labeling them as **(Taylor's Version)**, to show that she, and no one else, owned them. *Fearless (Taylor's Version)* was her first re-recording.

The **next-highest-grossing** concert ever was Elton John's Farewell Tour. He toured for five years. The Eras Tour lasted less than two.

Swift produced a concert film of the Eras Tour. She sold it directly to movie theaters, rather than letting a distributor—who would take part of her earnings—find buyers for her. Earning over **$261 million**, *Taylor Swift: The Eras Tour* became the highest-grossing concert or performance film of all time.

Extra Firsts!

In 1914, the US military asked Tiny Broadwick to demonstrate safe parachuting to its soldiers. This would help them survive if their planes crashed. Before one demonstration, Broadwick had to cut the cord that automatically opened her parachute. Then, she deployed her chute herself before jumping. She was the first person to make a freefall jump.

The first woman to participate at the Olympics—and also win an Olympic medal—was Swiss-American Helene de Pourtales. She was part of a Swiss yacht crew during the 1900 Games. It was the first time women were allowed in the Olympics. De Pourtales and 21 other women competed against 975 men.

Annie Edson Taylor barreled over Niagara Falls. Maria Spelterini walked! In 1876, 23-year-old Spelterini became the only woman to cross over Niagara Gorge on a tightrope. Instead of shoes, she wore peach baskets on her feet. The next week, she did it blindfolded, and later, with her arms and legs handcuffed together.

During the 2020 Tokyo Olympics, 49 percent of the participants were women. This was the first time the number of men and women was nearly equal. The Paris 2024 Olympics will be the first to have an equal quota of male and female athletes.

Read More

Arnéz, Lynda. *Be a Pro Skateboarder*. Buffalo, NY: Gareth Stevens Publishing, 2024.

Rodriguez, Cindy. *The Mount Everest Disaster of 1996*. North Mankato, MN: Capstone Press, an imprint of Capstone, 2023.

Staats, Ann McCallum. *Thrill Seekers: 15 Remarkable Women in Extreme Sports*. Chicago: Chicago Review Press, 2021.

1992: Junko Tabei becomes the first woman to complete the Seven Summits.

1995: The first X Games is held, featuring six events for women in extreme sports.

2001: Susan Helms becomes the first woman to live and work aboard the International Space Station.